THIS PRAYER JOURNAL BL

PRAY ABOUT IT!

Prayer makes you feel better!!!

LET'S PRAY!

For Kids

120 Day Prayer Journal

With 60 Bible Verses

Katie Mac Print

Scripture quotations are taken from the Holy Bible, New Living Translation,
copyright © 1996, 2004, 2007 by Tyndale House Foundation.
Used by permission of Tyndale House Publishers, Inc.,
Carol Stream, Illinois 60188. All rights reserved.

DEAR GOD!

_____
DATE

The LORD is good to everyone.

Psalms 145:9

LORD HELP ME DO THIS TODAY:

_____
_____
_____

TODAY I'M PRAYING ABOUT:
(WRITE OR DRAW)

TODAY I FEEL...

WHAT I THINK ABOUT TODAYS BIBLE VERSE:

1. _____

2. _____

AMEN!

DEAR GOD!

_____
DATE

HI

TODAY I'D LIKE TO PRAY ABOUT:

(WRITE OR DRAW)

TODAY I FEEL...

TODAY I'M THANKFUL FOR:

1. _____

2. _____

TODAY I'M PRAYING FOR THESE PEOPLE:

_____

_____

AMEN!

DEAR GOD!

_____
DATE

TODAY I FEEL...

May the LORD bless you
and protect you.

Numbers 6:24

PEOPLE I'M THANKFUL
FOR TODAY:

THIS MADE ME LAUGH TODAY:

_____

_____

TODAY I'M PRAYING ABOUT:
(WRITE OR DRAW)

AMEN!

DEAR GOD!

_____
DATE

TODAY I'M THANKFUL FOR:

1. _____

2. _____

THE BEST PART OF MY DAY:

_____

_____

TODAY I'M
PRAYING ABOUT:
(WRITE OR DRAW)

TODAY I FEEL...

AMEN!

DEAR GOD!

_____
DATE

You are the God who
sees me. Genesis 16:13

LORD HELP ME DO THIS TODAY:

_____
_____

TODAY I'M
PRAYING ABOUT:
(WRITE OR DRAW)

TODAY I FEEL...

WHAT I THINK ABOUT
TODAYS BIBLE VERSE:

1. _____

2. _____

AMEN!

DEAR GOD!

_____

HI

TODAY I'D LIKE TO PRAY ABOUT:

(WRITE OR DRAW)

TODAY I FEEL...

TODAY I'M THANKFUL FOR:

1. _____

2. _____

TODAY I'M PRAYING FOR THESE PEOPLE:

_____

_____

AMEN!

DEAR GOD!

_____
DATE

*Always be full of
joy in the Lord.*
Philippians 4:4

PEOPLE I'M THANKFUL
FOR TODAY:

THIS MADE ME LAUGH TODAY:

_____

_____

TODAY I'M PRAYING ABOUT:
(WRITE OR DRAW)

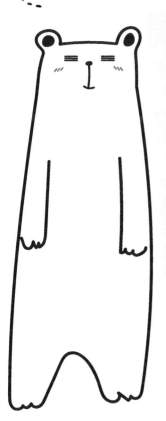

AMEN!

DEAR GOD!

_____
DATE

TODAY I'M THANKFUL FOR:

1. _____

2. _____

THE BEST PART OF MY DAY:

_____

_____

TODAY I'M PRAYING ABOUT:
(WRITE OR DRAW)

TODAY I FEEL...

AMEN!

DEAR GOD!

Let everything that
breathes sing praises to
the Lord.   Psalm 150:6

LORD HELP ME DO THIS TODAY:

_____

_____

TODAY I'M
PRAYING ABOUT:
(WRITE OR DRAW)

TODAY I FEEL...

WHAT I THINK ABOUT
TODAYS BIBLE VERSE:

1. _____

2. _____

AMEN!

DEAR GOD!

TODAY I'D LIKE TO PRAY ABOUT:

(WRITE OR DRAW)

HI

TODAY I FEEL...

TODAY I'M THANKFUL FOR:

1. _____

2. _____

TODAY I'M PRAYING FOR THESE PEOPLE:

_____

_____

AMEN!

DEAR GOD!

_____
DATE

TODAY I FEEL...

Children are a
gift from the Lord.

Psalm 127:3

PEOPLE I'M THANKFUL
FOR TODAY:

THIS MADE ME LAUGH TODAY:

_____

_____

TODAY I'M PRAYING ABOUT:
(WRITE OR DRAW)

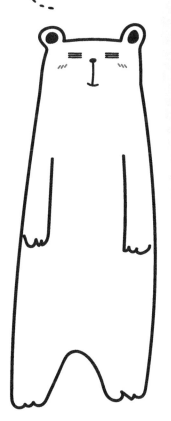

AMEN!

DEAR GOD!

_____
DATE

TODAY I'M THANKFUL FOR:

1. _____

2. _____

THE BEST PART OF MY DAY:

_____

_____

TODAY I'M PRAYING ABOUT:
(WRITE OR DRAW)

TODAY I FEEL...

AMEN!

DEAR GOD!

We love each other
because he loved us first.

1 John 4:19

LORD HELP ME DO THIS TODAY:

_____

_____

TODAY I'M
PRAYING ABOUT:
(WRITE OR DRAW)

TODAY I FEEL...

WHAT I THINK ABOUT
TODAYS BIBLE VERSE:

1. _____

2. _____

AMEN!

DEAR GOD!

_____
DATE

TODAY I'D LIKE TO PRAY ABOUT:

(WRITE OR DRAW)

HI

TODAY I FEEL...

TODAY I'M THANKFUL FOR:

1. _____

2. _____

TODAY I'M PRAYING FOR THESE PEOPLE:

_____

_____

AMEN!

DEAR GOD!

_____
DATE

Do to others as you would
like them to do to you.

Luke 6:31

PEOPLE I'M THANKFUL
FOR TODAY:

THIS MADE ME LAUGH TODAY:

_____

_____

TODAY I'M PRAYING ABOUT:
(WRITE OR DRAW)

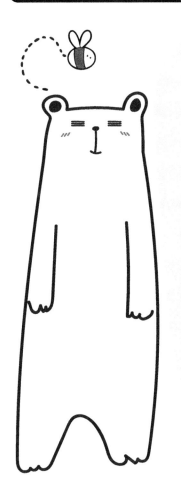

AMEN!

DEAR GOD!

_____
DATE

TODAY I'M THANKFUL FOR:

1. _____

2. _____

THE BEST PART OF MY DAY:

_____

_____

TODAY I'M
PRAYING ABOUT:
(WRITE OR DRAW)

TODAY I FEEL...

AMEN!

DEAR GOD!

_____
DATE

This is the day the
Lord has made.

Psalm 118:24

LORD HELP ME DO THIS TODAY:

_____

_____

TODAY I'M
PRAYING ABOUT:
(WRITE OR DRAW)

TODAY I FEEL...

WHAT I THINK ABOUT
TODAYS BIBLE VERSE:

1. _____

2. _____

AMEN!

DEAR GOD!

HI

TODAY I'D LIKE TO PRAY ABOUT:

(WRITE OR DRAW)

TODAY I FEEL...

TODAY I'M THANKFUL FOR:

1. _____

2. _____

TODAY I'M PRAYING FOR THESE PEOPLE:

_____

_____

AMEN!

DEAR GOD!

_____
DATE

TODAY I FEEL...

Be kind to each other.

Ephesians 4:32

PEOPLE I'M THANKFUL FOR TODAY:

THIS MADE ME LAUGH TODAY:

_____

_____

TODAY I'M PRAYING ABOUT:
(WRITE OR DRAW)

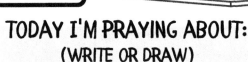

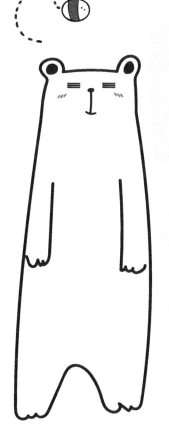

AMEN!

DEAR GOD!

_____
DATE

TODAY I'M THANKFUL FOR:

1. _____

2. _____

```
┌─────────────────────────────────────────┐
│          THE BEST PART OF MY DAY:         │
│                                           │
│   _____  │
│                                           │
│   _____  │
└─────────────────────────────────────────┘
```

TODAY I'M PRAYING ABOUT:
(WRITE OR DRAW)

TODAY I FEEL...

AMEN!

DEAR GOD!

_____
DATE

Love one another.

1 John 3:23

LORD HELP ME DO THIS TODAY:

_____
_____
_____

TODAY I'M PRAYING ABOUT:
(WRITE OR DRAW)

TODAY I FEEL...

WHAT I THINK ABOUT
TODAYS BIBLE VERSE:

1. _____

2. _____

AMEN!

DEAR GOD!

_____
DATE

TODAY I'D LIKE TO PRAY ABOUT:
(WRITE OR DRAW)

HI

TODAY I FEEL...

TODAY I'M THANKFUL FOR:

1. _____

2. _____

TODAY I'M PRAYING FOR THESE PEOPLE:

_____

_____

AMEN!

DEAR GOD!

_____
DATE

TODAY I FEEL...

But when I am afraid, I will put my trust in You.

Psalm 56:3

PEOPLE I'M THANKFUL FOR TODAY:

THIS MADE ME LAUGH TODAY:

_____

_____

TODAY I'M PRAYING ABOUT:
(WRITE OR DRAW)

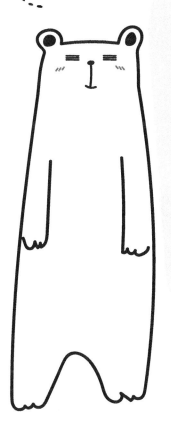

AMEN!

DEAR GOD!

_____
DATE

TODAY I'M THANKFUL FOR:

1. _____

2. _____

THE BEST PART OF MY DAY:

_____

_____

TODAY I'M
PRAYING ABOUT:
(WRITE OR DRAW)

TODAY I FEEL...

AMEN!

DEAR GOD!

_____
DATE

Children, always obey
your parents.
Colossians 3:20

LORD HELP ME DO THIS TODAY:

_____

_____

TODAY I'M
PRAYING ABOUT:
(WRITE OR DRAW)

TODAY I FEEL...

**WHAT I THINK ABOUT
TODAYS BIBLE VERSE:**

1. _____

2. _____

AMEN!

DEAR GOD!

_____
DATE

TODAY I'D LIKE TO PRAY ABOUT:

(WRITE OR DRAW)

HI

TODAY I FEEL...

TODAY I'M THANKFUL FOR:

1. _____

2. _____

TODAY I'M PRAYING FOR THESE PEOPLE:

_____

_____

AMEN!

DEAR GOD!

_____
DATE

TODAY I FEEL...

Do not be afraid,
for I am with you.
Isaiah 43:5

PEOPLE I'M THANKFUL
FOR TODAY:

THIS MADE ME LAUGH TODAY:

_____

_____

TODAY I'M PRAYING ABOUT:
(WRITE OR DRAW)

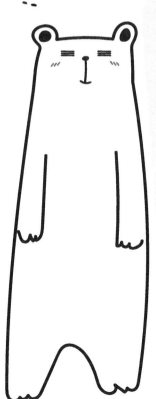

AMEN!

DEAR GOD!

_____

DATE

TODAY I'M THANKFUL FOR:

1. _____

2. _____

THE BEST PART OF MY DAY:

_____

_____

TODAY I'M PRAYING ABOUT:
(WRITE OR DRAW)

TODAY I FEEL...

AMEN!

DEAR GOD!

In the beginning God created the heavens and the earth. Genesis 1:1

LORD HELP ME DO THIS TODAY:

_____

_____

TODAY I'M PRAYING ABOUT:
(WRITE OR DRAW)

TODAY I FEEL...

WHAT I THINK ABOUT TODAYS BIBLE VERSE:

1. _____

2. _____

AMEN!

DEAR GOD!

_____

HI

TODAY I'D LIKE TO PRAY ABOUT:

(WRITE OR DRAW)

TODAY I FEEL...

TODAY I'M THANKFUL FOR:

1. _____

2. _____

TODAY I'M PRAYING FOR THESE PEOPLE:

_____

_____

AMEN!

DEAR GOD!

_____
DATE

TODAY I FEEL...

For I know the plans I have for you, says the Lord.

Jeremiah 29:11

PEOPLE I'M THANKFUL FOR TODAY:

THIS MADE ME LAUGH TODAY:

_____

_____

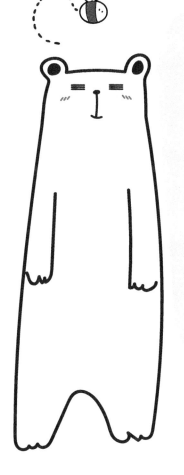

TODAY I'M PRAYING ABOUT:
(WRITE OR DRAW)

AMEN!

DEAR GOD!

_____
DATE

TODAY I'M THANKFUL FOR:

1. _____

2. _____

THE BEST PART OF MY DAY:

_____

_____

TODAY I'M
PRAYING ABOUT:
(WRITE OR DRAW)

TODAY I FEEL...

AMEN!

DEAR GOD!

Let the message about
Christ, in all its richness,
      fill your lives.   Colossians 3:16

LORD HELP ME DO THIS TODAY:

_____

_____

TODAY I'M
PRAYING ABOUT:
(WRITE OR DRAW)

TODAY I FEEL...

WHAT I THINK ABOUT
TODAYS BIBLE VERSE:

1. _____

2. _____   AMEN!

DEAR GOD!

TODAY I'D LIKE TO PRAY ABOUT:

(WRITE OR DRAW)

HI

TODAY I FEEL...

TODAY I'M THANKFUL FOR:

1. _____

2. _____

TODAY I'M PRAYING FOR THESE PEOPLE:

_____

_____

AMEN!

DEAR GOD!

_____
DATE

Jesus Christ is the
same yesterday, today
and forever.

Hebrews 13:8

PEOPLE I'M THANKFUL
FOR TODAY:

THIS MADE ME LAUGH TODAY:

_____

_____

TODAY I'M PRAYING ABOUT:
(WRITE OR DRAW)

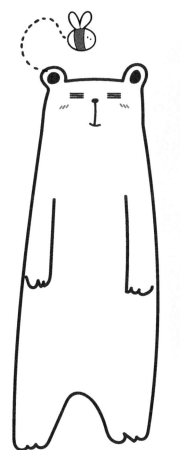

AMEN!

DEAR GOD!

_____
DATE

TODAY I'M THANKFUL FOR:

1. _____

2. _____

THE BEST PART OF MY DAY:

_____

_____

TODAY I'M PRAYING ABOUT:
(WRITE OR DRAW)

TODAY I FEEL...

AMEN!

DEAR GOD!

_____
DATE

Trust in the Lord with
   all your heart.
Proverbs 3:5

LORD HELP ME DO THIS TODAY:

_____

_____

TODAY I'M
PRAYING ABOUT:
(WRITE OR DRAW)

TODAY I FEEL...

WHAT I THINK ABOUT
TODAYS BIBLE VERSE:

1. _____

2. _____

AMEN!

DEAR GOD!

HI

TODAY I'D LIKE TO PRAY ABOUT:

(WRITE OR DRAW)

TODAY I FEEL...

TODAY I'M THANKFUL FOR:

1. _____

2. _____

TODAY I'M PRAYING FOR THESE PEOPLE:

_____

_____

AMEN!

DEAR GOD!

_____
DATE

TODAY I FEEL...

You can pray for anything.

Matthew 21:22

PEOPLE I'M THANKFUL
FOR TODAY:

THIS MADE ME LAUGH TODAY:

_____
_____

TODAY I'M PRAYING ABOUT:
(WRITE OR DRAW)

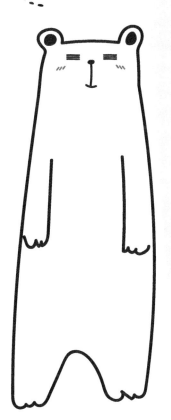

AMEN!

DEAR GOD!

_____
DATE

TODAY I'M THANKFUL FOR:

1. _____

2. _____

THE BEST PART OF MY DAY:

_____

_____

TODAY I'M
PRAYING ABOUT:
(WRITE OR DRAW)

TODAY I FEEL...

AMEN!

DEAR GOD!

_____
DATE

Love your neighbor as
yourself.

Matthew 22:39

LORD HELP ME DO THIS TODAY:

_____

_____

TODAY I'M
PRAYING ABOUT:
(WRITE OR DRAW)

TODAY I FEEL...

WHAT I THINK ABOUT
TODAYS BIBLE VERSE:

1. _____

2. _____

AMEN!

DEAR GOD!

_____

DATE

HI

TODAY I'D LIKE TO PRAY ABOUT:

(WRITE OR DRAW)

TODAY I FEEL...

TODAY I'M THANKFUL FOR:

1. _____

2. _____

TODAY I'M PRAYING FOR THESE PEOPLE:

_____

_____

AMEN!

DEAR GOD!

_____
DATE

TODAY I FEEL...

How precious are your thoughts about me, O God.

Psalm 139:17

PEOPLE I'M THANKFUL FOR TODAY:

THIS MADE ME LAUGH TODAY:

_____

_____

TODAY I'M PRAYING ABOUT:
(WRITE OR DRAW)

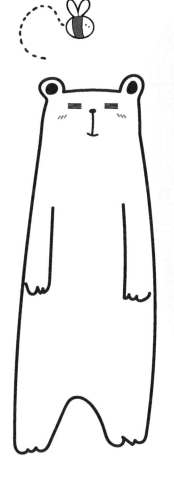

AMEN!

DEAR GOD!

_____
DATE

TODAY I'M THANKFUL FOR:

1. _____

2. _____

THE BEST PART OF MY DAY:

_____

_____

TODAY I'M
PRAYING ABOUT:
(WRITE OR DRAW)

TODAY I FEEL...

AMEN!

DEAR GOD!

_____
DATE

Give thanks to the Lord,
   for he is good.
                    psalm 107:1

LORD HELP ME DO THIS TODAY:

_____

_____

_____

**TODAY I'M
PRAYING ABOUT:**
(WRITE OR DRAW)

TODAY I FEEL...

**WHAT I THINK ABOUT
TODAYS BIBLE VERSE:**

1. _____

2. _____

AMEN!

DEAR GOD!

HI

TODAY I'D LIKE TO PRAY ABOUT:

(WRITE OR DRAW)

TODAY I FEEL...

TODAY I'M THANKFUL FOR:

1. _____

2. _____

TODAY I'M PRAYING FOR THESE PEOPLE:

_____

_____

AMEN!

DEAR GOD!

_____
DATE

TODAY I FEEL...

Every word of God
proves true.

Proverbs 30:5

PEOPLE I'M THANKFUL
FOR TODAY:

THIS MADE ME LAUGH TODAY:

_____

_____

TODAY I'M PRAYING ABOUT:
(WRITE OR DRAW)

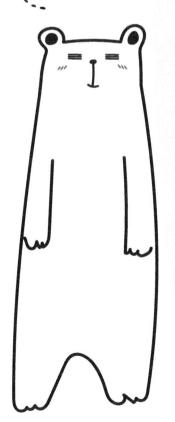

AMEN!

DEAR GOD!

_____
DATE

TODAY I'M THANKFUL FOR:

1. _____

2. _____

THE BEST PART OF MY DAY:

_____

_____

TODAY I'M PRAYING ABOUT:
(WRITE OR DRAW)

TODAY I FEEL...

AMEN!

DEAR GOD!

Children obey your parents
because you belong to the
Lord.   Ephesians 6:1

DATE _____

LORD HELP ME DO THIS TODAY:

_____
_____
_____

TODAY I'M
PRAYING ABOUT:
(WRITE OR DRAW)

TODAY I FEEL...

WHAT I THINK ABOUT
TODAYS BIBLE VERSE:

1. _____

2. _____

AMEN!

DEAR GOD! _____

HI

TODAY I'D LIKE TO PRAY ABOUT:

(WRITE OR DRAW)

TODAY I FEEL...

TODAY I'M THANKFUL FOR:

1. _____

2. _____

TODAY I'M PRAYING FOR THESE PEOPLE:

_____

_____

AMEN!

DEAR GOD!

_____
DATE

TODAY I FEEL...

And you must love the
Lord your God with all
your heart.

Deuteronomy 6:5

PEOPLE I'M THANKFUL
FOR TODAY:

THIS MADE ME LAUGH TODAY:

_____

_____

TODAY I'M PRAYING ABOUT:
(WRITE OR DRAW)

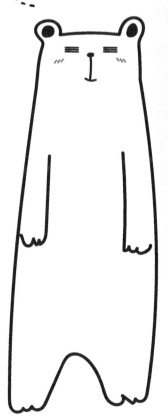

AMEN!

DEAR GOD!

_____
DATE

TODAY I'M THANKFUL FOR:

1. _____

2. _____

THE BEST PART OF MY DAY:

_____

_____

TODAY I'M PRAYING ABOUT:
(WRITE OR DRAW)

TODAY I FEEL...

AMEN!

DEAR GOD!

The heavens proclaim
the glory of God.

Psalm 19:1

LORD HELP ME DO THIS TODAY:

_____
_____

TODAY I'M PRAYING ABOUT:
(WRITE OR DRAW)

TODAY I FEEL...

WHAT I THINK ABOUT
TODAYS BIBLE VERSE:

1. _____

2. _____   **AMEN!**

DEAR GOD!

_____
DATE

TODAY I'D LIKE TO PRAY ABOUT:
(WRITE OR DRAW)

HI

TODAY I FEEL...

TODAY I'M THANKFUL FOR:

1. _____

2. _____

TODAY I'M PRAYING FOR THESE PEOPLE:

_____

_____

AMEN!

DEAR GOD! _____
DATE

You saw me before
I was born.

Psalm 139:16

PEOPLE I'M THANKFUL
FOR TODAY:

THIS MADE ME LAUGH TODAY:

_____

_____

TODAY I'M PRAYING ABOUT:
(WRITE OR DRAW)

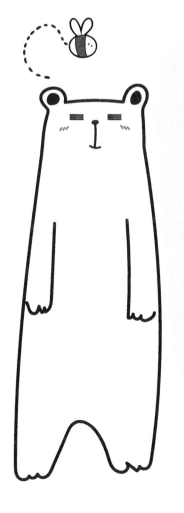

AMEN!

DEAR GOD!

_____
DATE

TODAY I'M THANKFUL FOR:

1. _____

2. _____

THE BEST PART OF MY DAY:

_____

_____

TODAY I'M
PRAYING ABOUT:
(WRITE OR DRAW)

TODAY I FEEL...

AMEN!

DEAR GOD!

DATE

Trust in the Lord
always. *Isaiah 26:4*

LORD HELP ME DO THIS TODAY:

_____

_____

TODAY I'M
PRAYING ABOUT:
(WRITE OR DRAW)

TODAY I FEEL...

WHAT I THINK ABOUT
TODAYS BIBLE VERSE:

1. _____

2. _____

AMEN!

DEAR GOD! _____

DATE

HI

TODAY I'D LIKE TO PRAY ABOUT:
(WRITE OR DRAW)

TODAY I FEEL...

TODAY I'M THANKFUL FOR:

1. _____

2. _____

TODAY I'M PRAYING FOR THESE PEOPLE:

_____

_____

AMEN!

DEAR GOD!

_____
DATE

TODAY I FEEL...

Forgive anyone who
offends you.

Colossians 3:13

PEOPLE I'M THANKFUL
FOR TODAY:

THIS MADE ME LAUGH TODAY:

_____

_____

TODAY I'M PRAYING ABOUT:
(WRITE OR DRAW)

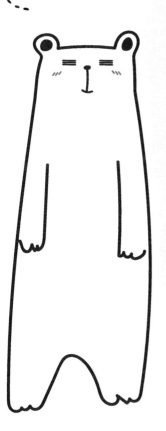

AMEN!

DEAR GOD!

_____
DATE

TODAY I'M THANKFUL FOR:

1. _____

2. _____

THE BEST PART OF MY DAY:

_____

_____

TODAY I'M PRAYING ABOUT:
(WRITE OR DRAW)

TODAY I FEEL...

AMEN!

DEAR GOD!

_____
DATE

You are the light of the world.

Matthew 5:14

LORD HELP ME DO THIS TODAY:

_____

_____

TODAY I'M PRAYING ABOUT:
(WRITE OR DRAW)

TODAY I FEEL...

WHAT I THINK ABOUT TODAYS BIBLE VERSE:

1. _____

2. _____

AMEN!

DEAR GOD!

_____

DATE

TODAY I'D LIKE TO PRAY ABOUT:

(WRITE OR DRAW)

HI

TODAY I FEEL...

TODAY I'M THANKFUL FOR:

1. _____

2. _____

TODAY I'M PRAYING FOR THESE PEOPLE:

_____

_____

AMEN!

DEAR GOD!

_____
DATE

TODAY I FEEL...

Be still and know
that I am God.

Psalm 46:10

PEOPLE I'M THANKFUL FOR TODAY:

THIS MADE ME LAUGH TODAY:

_____
_____

TODAY I'M PRAYING ABOUT:
(WRITE OR DRAW)

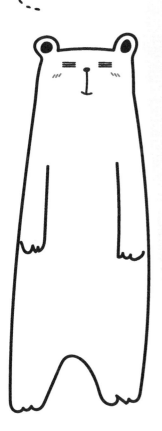

AMEN!

DEAR GOD!

_____
DATE

TODAY I'M THANKFUL FOR:

1. _____

2. _____

THE BEST PART OF MY DAY:

_____

_____

TODAY I'M PRAYING ABOUT:
(WRITE OR DRAW)

TODAY I FEEL...

AMEN!

DEAR GOD!

_____
DATE

My child, listen to what
I say.

Proverbs 2:1

LORD HELP ME DO THIS TODAY:

_____

_____

TODAY I'M
PRAYING ABOUT:
(WRITE OR DRAW)

TODAY I FEEL...

WHAT I THINK ABOUT
TODAYS BIBLE VERSE:

1. _____

2. _____   AMEN!

DEAR GOD!

HI

TODAY I'D LIKE TO PRAY ABOUT:

(WRITE OR DRAW)

TODAY I FEEL...

TODAY I'M THANKFUL FOR:

1. _____

2. _____

TODAY I'M PRAYING FOR THESE PEOPLE:

_____

_____

AMEN!

DEAR GOD! _____
DATE

TODAY I FEEL...

Fear God and obey
his commands.
Ecclesiastes 12:13

PEOPLE I'M THANKFUL
FOR TODAY:

THIS MADE ME LAUGH TODAY:

_____

_____

TODAY I'M PRAYING ABOUT:
(WRITE OR DRAW)

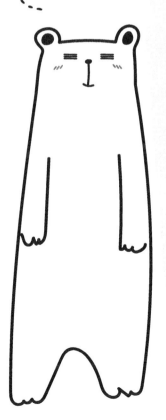

AMEN!

DEAR GOD!

_____
DATE

TODAY I'M THANKFUL FOR:

1. _____

2. _____

THE BEST PART OF MY DAY:

_____

_____

TODAY I'M
PRAYING ABOUT:
(WRITE OR DRAW)

TODAY I FEEL...

AMEN!

DEAR GOD!

_____
DATE

So God created human
beings in his own
image.   Genesis 1:27

LORD HELP ME DO THIS TODAY:

_____
_____

TODAY I'M
PRAYING ABOUT:
(WRITE OR DRAW)

TODAY I FEEL...

**WHAT I THINK ABOUT
TODAYS BIBLE VERSE:**

1. _____

2. _____   **AMEN!**

DEAR GOD!

DATE _____

TODAY I'D LIKE TO PRAY ABOUT:

(WRITE OR DRAW)

HI

TODAY I FEEL...

TODAY I'M THANKFUL FOR:

1. _____

2. _____

TODAY I'M PRAYING FOR THESE PEOPLE:

_____

_____

AMEN!

DEAR GOD!

_____
DATE

TODAY I FEEL...

Turn away from
evil and do good.

Psalm 34:14

PEOPLE I'M THANKFUL FOR TODAY:

THIS MADE ME LAUGH TODAY:

_____

_____

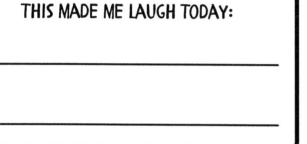

TODAY I'M PRAYING ABOUT:
(WRITE OR DRAW)

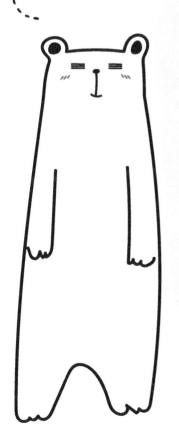

AMEN!

DEAR GOD!

_____
DATE

TODAY I'M THANKFUL FOR:

1. _____

2. _____

THE BEST PART OF MY DAY:

_____

_____

TODAY I'M PRAYING ABOUT:
(WRITE OR DRAW)

TODAY I FEEL...

AMEN!

DEAR GOD!

DATE _____

For I can do everything
through Christ, who
gives me strength. Philippians 4:13

LORD HELP ME DO THIS TODAY:

_____

_____

**TODAY I'M
PRAYING ABOUT:**
(WRITE OR DRAW)

TODAY I FEEL...

**WHAT I THINK ABOUT
TODAYS BIBLE VERSE:**

1. _____

2. _____

AMEN!

DEAR GOD!

_____
DATE

TODAY I'D LIKE TO PRAY ABOUT:

(WRITE OR DRAW)

HI

TODAY I FEEL...

😍 ☺️

😐 🙁

TODAY I'M THANKFUL FOR:

1. _____

2. _____

TODAY I'M PRAYING FOR THESE PEOPLE:

_____

_____

AMEN!

DEAR GOD!

_____
DATE

TODAY I FEEL...

Conquer evil by
doing good.

Romans 12:21

PEOPLE I'M THANKFUL FOR TODAY:

THIS MADE ME LAUGH TODAY:

_____

_____

TODAY I'M PRAYING ABOUT:
(WRITE OR DRAW)

AMEN!

DEAR GOD!

_____
DATE

TODAY I'M THANKFUL FOR:

1. _____

2. _____

THE BEST PART OF MY DAY:

_____

_____

TODAY I'M
PRAYING ABOUT:
(WRITE OR DRAW)

TODAY I FEEL...

AMEN!

DEAR GOD!

_____
DATE

You must have the same
attitude that Christ
Jesus had.   Philippians 2:5

LORD HELP ME DO THIS TODAY:

_____

_____

**TODAY I'M
PRAYING ABOUT:**
(WRITE OR DRAW)

TODAY I FEEL...

**WHAT I THINK ABOUT
TODAYS BIBLE VERSE:**

1. _____

2. _____   **AMEN!**

DEAR GOD!

_____
DATE

HI

TODAY I'D LIKE TO PRAY ABOUT:
(WRITE OR DRAW)

TODAY I FEEL...

TODAY I'M THANKFUL FOR:

1. _____

2. _____

TODAY I'M PRAYING FOR THESE PEOPLE:

_____

_____

AMEN!

DEAR GOD!

_____
DATE

TODAY I FEEL...

So let's not get tired of
doing what is good.

Galatians 6:9

PEOPLE I'M THANKFUL
FOR TODAY:

THIS MADE ME LAUGH TODAY:

_____

_____

TODAY I'M PRAYING ABOUT:
(WRITE OR DRAW)

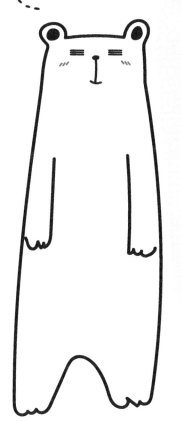

AMEN!

DEAR GOD!

_____
DATE

TODAY I'M THANKFUL FOR:

1. _____

2. _____

THE BEST PART OF MY DAY:

_____

_____

TODAY I'M PRAYING ABOUT:
(WRITE OR DRAW)

TODAY I FEEL...

AMEN!

DEAR GOD!

DATE _____

This is my command -
be strong and
courageous.   Joshua 1:9

LORD HELP ME DO THIS TODAY:

_____

_____

TODAY I'M
PRAYING ABOUT:
(WRITE OR DRAW)

TODAY I FEEL...

WHAT I THINK ABOUT
TODAYS BIBLE VERSE:

1. _____

2. _____

AMEN!

DEAR GOD!

_____

DATE

TODAY I'D LIKE TO PRAY ABOUT:

(WRITE OR DRAW)

HI

TODAY I FEEL...

TODAY I'M THANKFUL FOR:

1. _____

2. _____

TODAY I'M PRAYING FOR THESE PEOPLE:

_____

_____

AMEN!

DEAR GOD!

_____
DATE

TODAY I FEEL...

His faithful love
endures forever.

Psalm 136:1

PEOPLE I'M THANKFUL
FOR TODAY:

THIS MADE ME LAUGH TODAY:

_____

_____

TODAY I'M PRAYING ABOUT:
(WRITE OR DRAW)

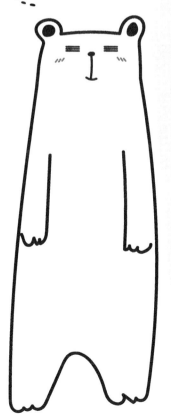

AMEN!

DEAR GOD!

DATE _____

TODAY I'M THANKFUL FOR:

1. _____

2. _____

THE BEST PART OF MY DAY:

_____

_____

TODAY I'M
PRAYING ABOUT:
(WRITE OR DRAW)

TODAY I FEEL...

AMEN!

DEAR GOD!

For all who are led by
the Spirit of God are
children of God. Romans 8:14

LORD HELP ME DO THIS TODAY:

_____

_____

TODAY I'M PRAYING ABOUT:
(WRITE OR DRAW)

TODAY I FEEL...

WHAT I THINK ABOUT
TODAYS BIBLE VERSE:

1. _____

2. _____

AMEN!

DEAR GOD! _____
DATE

TODAY I'D LIKE TO PRAY ABOUT:

(WRITE OR DRAW)

HI

TODAY I FEEL...

TODAY I'M THANKFUL FOR:

1. _____

2. _____

TODAY I'M PRAYING FOR THESE PEOPLE:

_____

_____

AMEN!

DEAR GOD!

_____
DATE

TODAY I FEEL...

God opposes the
proud but gives grace
to the humble.

1 Peter 5:5

PEOPLE I'M THANKFUL
FOR TODAY:

THIS MADE ME LAUGH TODAY:

_____

_____

TODAY I'M PRAYING ABOUT:
(WRITE OR DRAW)

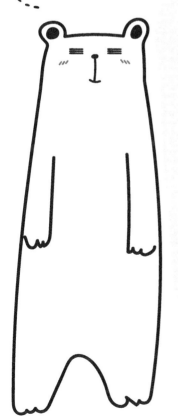

AMEN!

DEAR GOD!

_____
DATE

TODAY I'M THANKFUL FOR:

1. _____

2. _____

THE BEST PART OF MY DAY:

_____

_____

TODAY I'M PRAYING ABOUT:
(WRITE OR DRAW)

TODAY I FEEL...

AMEN!

DEAR GOD!

_____
DATE

Do everything without complaining and arguing.
Philippians 2:14

LORD HELP ME DO THIS TODAY:

_____

_____

TODAY I'M PRAYING ABOUT:
(WRITE OR DRAW)

TODAY I FEEL...

WHAT I THINK ABOUT TODAYS BIBLE VERSE:

1. _____

2. _____

AMEN!

DEAR GOD!

_____
DATE

TODAY I'D LIKE TO PRAY ABOUT:

(WRITE OR DRAW)

HI

TODAY I FEEL...

TODAY I'M THANKFUL FOR:

1. _____

2. _____

TODAY I'M PRAYING FOR THESE PEOPLE:

_____

_____

AMEN!

DEAR GOD!

_____
DATE

TODAY I FEEL...

I knew you before I formed you in your mother's womb. *Jeremiah 1:5*

PEOPLE I'M THANKFUL FOR TODAY:

THIS MADE ME LAUGH TODAY:

_____

_____

TODAY I'M PRAYING ABOUT:
(WRITE OR DRAW)

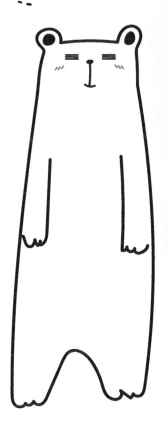

AMEN!

DEAR GOD!

_____
DATE

TODAY I'M THANKFUL FOR:

1. _____

2. _____

THE BEST PART OF MY DAY:

_____

_____

TODAY I'M
PRAYING ABOUT:
(WRITE OR DRAW)

TODAY I FEEL...

AMEN!

DEAR GOD!

_____
DATE

For everyone who calls
on the name of the Lord
will be saved. Romans 10:13

LORD HELP ME DO THIS TODAY:

_____

_____

TODAY I'M
PRAYING ABOUT:
(WRITE OR DRAW)

TODAY I FEEL...

WHAT I THINK ABOUT
TODAYS BIBLE VERSE:

1. _____

2. _____   AMEN!

DEAR GOD!

_____

DATE

TODAY I'D LIKE TO PRAY ABOUT:

(WRITE OR DRAW)

HI

TODAY I FEEL...

TODAY I'M THANKFUL FOR:

1. _____

2. _____

TODAY I'M PRAYING FOR THESE PEOPLE:

_____

_____

AMEN!

DEAR GOD!

_____
DATE

And let the peace that
comes from Christ rule in
your hearts.

Colossians 3:15

**PEOPLE I'M THANKFUL
FOR TODAY:**

THIS MADE ME LAUGH TODAY:

_____

_____

TODAY I'M PRAYING ABOUT:
(WRITE OR DRAW)

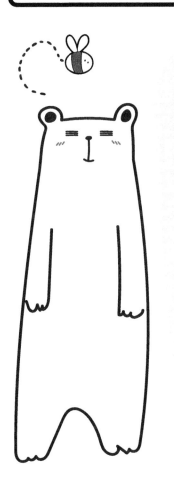

AMEN!

DEAR GOD!

_____
DATE

TODAY I'M THANKFUL FOR:

1. _____

2. _____

```
┌─────────────────────────────────────┐
│         THE BEST PART OF MY DAY:     │
│                                      │
│   _____    │
│                                      │
│   _____    │
└─────────────────────────────────────┘
```

TODAY I'M
PRAYING ABOUT:
(WRITE OR DRAW)

TODAY I FEEL...

AMEN!

DEAR GOD!

Remember, the Lord
forgave you, so you must
forgive others. Colossians 3:13

LORD HELP ME DO THIS TODAY:

_____

_____

TODAY I'M
PRAYING ABOUT:
(WRITE OR DRAW)

TODAY I FEEL...

WHAT I THINK ABOUT
TODAYS BIBLE VERSE:

1. _____

2. _____   AMEN!

DEAR GOD!

_____
DATE

TODAY I'D LIKE TO PRAY ABOUT:
(WRITE OR DRAW)

TODAY I FEEL...

TODAY I'M THANKFUL FOR:

1. _____

2. _____

TODAY I'M PRAYING FOR THESE PEOPLE:

_____

_____

AMEN!

DEAR GOD!

_____
DATE

TODAY I FEEL...

And do everything
with love.

1 Corinthians 16:14

PEOPLE I'M THANKFUL
FOR TODAY:

THIS MADE ME LAUGH TODAY:

_____

_____

TODAY I'M PRAYING ABOUT:
(WRITE OR DRAW)

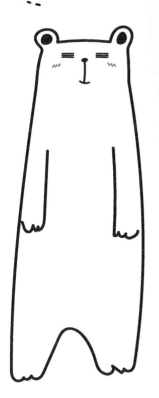

AMEN!

DEAR GOD!

_____
DATE

TODAY I'M THANKFUL FOR:

1. _____

2. _____

THE BEST PART OF MY DAY:

_____

_____

TODAY I'M
PRAYING ABOUT:
(WRITE OR DRAW)

TODAY I FEEL...

AMEN!

DEAR GOD!

If God is for us,
who can ever be
against us?   Romans 8:31

DATE _____

LORD HELP ME DO THIS TODAY:

_____

_____

TODAY I'M
PRAYING ABOUT:
(WRITE OR DRAW)

TODAY I FEEL...

WHAT I THINK ABOUT
TODAYS BIBLE VERSE:

1. _____

2. _____

AMEN!

DEAR GOD!

_____

TODAY I'D LIKE TO PRAY ABOUT:

(WRITE OR DRAW)

HI

TODAY I FEEL...

TODAY I'M THANKFUL FOR:

1. _____

2. _____

TODAY I'M PRAYING FOR THESE PEOPLE:

_____

_____

AMEN!

DEAR GOD!

_____
DATE

TODAY I FEEL...

Your word is a lamp to guide my feet and a light for my path.

Psalm 119:105

THIS MADE ME LAUGH TODAY:

_____

_____

PEOPLE I'M THANKFUL FOR TODAY:

TODAY I'M PRAYING ABOUT:
(WRITE OR DRAW)

AMEN!

DEAR GOD!

_____
DATE

TODAY I'M THANKFUL FOR:

1. _____

2. _____

THE BEST PART OF MY DAY:

_____

_____

TODAY I'M PRAYING ABOUT:
(WRITE OR DRAW)

TODAY I FEEL...

AMEN!

DEAR GOD!

DATE _____

Anyone who belongs to
Christ has become a new
person. 2 Corinthians 5:17

LORD HELP ME DO THIS TODAY:

_____

_____

TODAY I'M
PRAYING ABOUT:
(WRITE OR DRAW)

TODAY I FEEL...

WHAT I THINK ABOUT
TODAYS BIBLE VERSE:

1. _____

2. _____

AMEN!

DEAR GOD!

_____
DATE

HI

TODAY I'D LIKE TO PRAY ABOUT:
(WRITE OR DRAW)

TODAY I FEEL...

TODAY I'M THANKFUL FOR:

1. _____

2. _____

TODAY I'M PRAYING FOR THESE PEOPLE:

_____

_____

AMEN!

DEAR GOD!

_____
DATE

TODAY I FEEL...

I am leaving you with a gift - peace of mind and heart.

John 14:27

PEOPLE I'M THANKFUL FOR TODAY:

THIS MADE ME LAUGH TODAY:

_____

_____

TODAY I'M PRAYING ABOUT:
(WRITE OR DRAW)

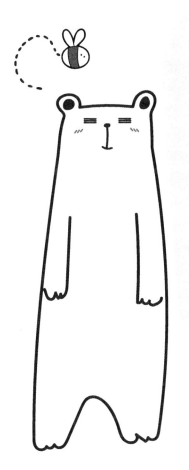

AMEN!

DEAR GOD!

_____
DATE

TODAY I'M THANKFUL FOR:

1. _____

2. _____

THE BEST PART OF MY DAY:
_____
_____

TODAY I'M PRAYING ABOUT:
(WRITE OR DRAW)

TODAY I FEEL...

AMEN!

DEAR GOD!

_____
DATE

I am always with you.

Matthew 28:20

LORD HELP ME DO THIS TODAY:

_____

_____

_____

TODAY I'M
PRAYING ABOUT:
(WRITE OR DRAW)

TODAY I FEEL...

WHAT I THINK ABOUT
TODAYS BIBLE VERSE:

1. _____

2. _____

AMEN!

DEAR GOD!

DATE _____

HI

TODAY I'D LIKE TO PRAY ABOUT:
(WRITE OR DRAW)

TODAY I FEEL...

TODAY I'M THANKFUL FOR:

1. _____

2. _____

TODAY I'M PRAYING FOR THESE PEOPLE:

_____

_____

AMEN!

DEAR GOD!

_____
DATE

TODAY I FEEL...

The Lord is like a Father
to his children.

Psalm 103:13

PEOPLE I'M THANKFUL
FOR TODAY:

THIS MADE ME LAUGH TODAY:

_____

_____

TODAY I'M PRAYING ABOUT:
(WRITE OR DRAW)

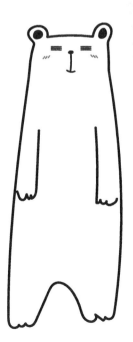

AMEN!

DEAR GOD!

_____
DATE

TODAY I'M THANKFUL FOR:

1. _____

2. _____

THE BEST PART OF MY DAY:

_____

_____

TODAY I'M
PRAYING ABOUT:
(WRITE OR DRAW)

TODAY I FEEL...

AMEN!

DEAR GOD!

_____
DATE

He has given us the Holy
Spirit to fill our hearts
with his love. Romans 5:5

LORD HELP ME DO THIS TODAY:

_____
_____
_____

**TODAY I'M
PRAYING ABOUT:**
(WRITE OR DRAW)

TODAY I FEEL...

**WHAT I THINK ABOUT
TODAYS BIBLE VERSE:**

1. _____

2. _____

AMEN!

DEAR GOD!

_____
DATE

HI

TODAY I'D LIKE TO PRAY ABOUT:

(WRITE OR DRAW)

TODAY I FEEL...

TODAY I'M THANKFUL FOR:

1. _____

2. _____

TODAY I'M PRAYING FOR THESE PEOPLE:

_____

_____

AMEN!

DEAR GOD!

_____
DATE

TODAY I FEEL...

Let us continue to love
one another.
1 John 4:7

**PEOPLE I'M THANKFUL
FOR TODAY:**

THIS MADE ME LAUGH TODAY:

_____

_____

TODAY I'M PRAYING ABOUT:
(WRITE OR DRAW)

AMEN!

DEAR GOD!

_____
DATE

TODAY I'M THANKFUL FOR:

1. _____

2. _____

THE BEST PART OF MY DAY:

_____

_____

TODAY I'M
PRAYING ABOUT:
(WRITE OR DRAW)

TODAY I FEEL...

AMEN!

DEAR GOD!

God is love.
1 John 4:16

LORD HELP ME DO THIS TODAY:

_____

_____

TODAY I'M
PRAYING ABOUT:
(WRITE OR DRAW)

TODAY I FEEL...

WHAT I THINK ABOUT
TODAYS BIBLE VERSE:

1. _____

2. _____ AMEN!

DEAR GOD!

_____
DATE

TODAY I'D LIKE TO PRAY ABOUT:
(WRITE OR DRAW)

HI

TODAY I FEEL...

TODAY I'M THANKFUL FOR:

1. _____

2. _____

TODAY I'M PRAYING FOR THESE PEOPLE:

_____

_____

AMEN!

DEAR GOD!

_____
DATE

TODAY I FEEL...

Let all that I am
praise the Lord.

Psalm 103:22

PEOPLE I'M THANKFUL
FOR TODAY:

THIS MADE ME LAUGH TODAY:

_____

_____

TODAY I'M PRAYING ABOUT:
(WRITE OR DRAW)

AMEN!

DEAR GOD!

_____
DATE

TODAY I'M THANKFUL FOR:

1. _____

2. _____

```
THE BEST PART OF MY DAY:

_____

_____
```

TODAY I'M
PRAYING ABOUT:
(WRITE OR DRAW)

TODAY I FEEL...

AMEN!

Printed in Great Britain
by Amazon

83491731R00072